THE WARDROBE ENSEMBLE

The Wardrobe Ensemble is a Bristol-based group of theatre artists working together to make and tour new plays. They explore the big ideas of our time through intimate human stories and bold imagery. They consist of nine core members and a constantly growing community of associate artists, and work as a democratic devising ensemble wherein every member contributes to the research, writing, structuring and performing of a show, creating a unique, shared theatrical language and aesthetic from show to show. They have made a variety of shows for all ages, and at the heart of all their work is a desire to tell a compelling story in a visually engaging and inventive way.

The Wardrobe Ensemble has made nine full company shows, *RIOT, 33, 1972: The Future of Sex, Education, Education, Education, South Western, The Last of the Pelican Daughters, The Great Gatsby* and *WINNERS*. In 2021 they opened The Theatre on the Downs, a pop-up theatre space in Bristol which programmed thirty-five South-West artists and welcomed over 6500 audience members.

The company has also made five shows for younger years: *The Star Seekers, The Time Seekers, The Deep Sea Seekers, Little Tim and the Brave Sea Captain* and *Princess Smartypants*. In 2018, *The Star Seekers* played at the National Theatre for four weeks. The company have also made six shows for families: *Robin Hood: Legend of the Forgotten Forest* (Christmas 2021 co-production with Bristol Old Vic), *Eliza and the Wild Swans, Edgar and the Land of Lost, Eloise and the Curse of the Golden Whisk, The Forever Machine* and *The Wind in the Willows*.

Their shows have been performed at the National Theatre, Old Vic, Southbank Centre, Almeida, Trafalgar Studios, Bristol Old Vic, Northern Stage and abroad at Jack, New York.

In 2023 they launched a BA in Acting & Devised Theatre in collaboration with Bristol School of Acting.

www.thewardrobeensemble.com

The Wardrobe Ensemble

PARTY SEASON

NICK HERN BOOKS

London

www.nickhernbooks.co.uk

A Nick Hern Book

Party Season first published in Great Britain in 2026 as a paperback original by
Nick Hern Books Limited, The Glasshouse, 49a Goldhawk Road, London W12 8QP

Party Season copyright © 2026 The Wardrobe Ensemble

The Wardrobe Ensemble has asserted their moral right to be identified as the authors of
this work

Cover image: photography by Matt Crockett; design by Rebecca Pitt

Designed and typeset by Nick Hern Books, London
Printed in the UK by Mimeo Ltd, Huntingdon, Cambridgeshire PE29 6XX

A CIP catalogue record for this book is available from the British Library

ISBN 978 1 83904 598 1

CAUTION   All rights whatsoever in this play are strictly reserved. Requests to
reproduce the text in whole or in part should be addressed to the publisher. This book
may not be used, in whole or in part, for the development or training of artificial
intelligence technologies or systems.

Performing Rights   Applications for performance by amateurs or professionals,
including readings and excerpts, in the English language throughout the world should
be addressed, in the first instance, to the Performing Rights Department, Nick Hern
Books, The Glasshouse, 49a Goldhawk Road, London W12 8QP,
tel +44 (0)20 8749 4953, *email* rights@nickhernbooks.co.uk, except as follows:

Australia: ORiGiN Theatrical, Level 1, 213 Clarence Street, Sydney NSW 2000,
tel +61 (2) 8514 5201, *email* enquiries@originmusic.com.au,
web www.origintheatrical.com.au

New Zealand: Play Bureau, 20 Rua Street, Mangapapa, Gisborne, 4010,
tel +64 21 258 3998, *email* info@playbureau.com

No performance of any kind may be given unless a licence has been obtained.
Applications should be made before rehearsals begin. Publication of this play does
not necessarily indicate its availability for amateur performance.

www.nickhernbooks.co.uk/environmental-policy

Nick Hern Books' authorised representative in the EU is
Easy Access System Europe – Mustamäe tee 50, 10621 Tallinn, Estonia
email gpsr.requests@easproject.com

Party Season was first performed at the Royal & Derngate, Northampton, on 2 April 2026, before touring the UK. The cast and creative team were as follows:

DEVISORS

XANDER	Tom England
MARGOT/SIMONE/MAYA	Kerry Lovell
BEA	Fowzia Madar
CELIA	Jesse Meadows
ENTERTAINER/FELIX	James Newton
KANE/AONGHUS	Jacade Simpson
DAVID	Ben Vardy

Additional Devising by
Oliver Alvin-Wilson, Julia Cranney, Ben Grant, Alice Lamb, Joseph Langdon, Sara Lessore, Sophia Oriogun-Williams & Miray Sidhom

CREATIVE TEAM

Co-Directors	Helena Seneca
	& Jesse Jones
Set & Costume Designer	Bronia Housman
Sound Designer	Beth Duke
Lighting Designer	Chris Swain
Lead Writer	James Newton
Dramaturg	Tom Brennan
Trainee Assistant Director	Gracie Eve
Assistant Designer	Miranda Cattermole
Company Stage Manager	Rachel Bell
Stage Manager on the Book	Holly Beth
Assistant Stage Manager	Seren Tuson
Trainee Assistant Stage Manager	Bryony Bishop
Touring Production Manager	Tom Crosley-Thorne
TWE Producer	Hannah Smith
TWE Engagement Producer	Emily Greenslade
TWE Trainee Assistant Producer	Ben Henry Lamb

PRODUCTION TEAM

Deputy CEO *(Producing & Programming)*	Holly Gladwell
Producer	Remy Moynes
Production Manager	Claire Hardacre
Producing & Programming Assistant	Laura Barton
Wardrobe Team	Victoria Youngson & Abbie Pillet
Workshop Team	Sam Wilcox, Andy Pike & Matt Duffy
Scenic Art Team	Bronwen Herdman
Props & Furniture	Darren Abel
Royal Stage Team	James Chapman, Chris Rice & Dhiren Basu
Royal Technical Team	Jo McIlwaine, Ethan Monk & JB Pike

A Wardrobe Ensemble, Royal & Derngate, Northampton and Lowry co-production. *Party Season* was developed with the support of the National Theatre's Generate programme.

Directors' Note

Our work is often inspired by a collective reflection on where we are in our lives as an ensemble.

This play comes from a moment of transition within us, as several of us have become parents, and found ourselves navigating the joyful and disorientating shift that brings. It's a time that reshapes everything: your routines, your relationships, and your sense of who you thought you were.

Becoming a parent also has a way of sending you backwards. To your own childhood. Your upbringing. Your relationship with your parents. It asks questions about what you might carry forward, and what you'd rather leave behind.

The starting point for this show was a real-life weekend of back-to-back children's parties in Bristol. From there, the play probes the feelings beneath the noise, chaos and small talk, reflecting on how these environments can evoke feelings of loneliness or isolation, and how they make you question the version of yourself you bring into these new social settings.

Our process is always shaped by the people in the room. And as ever, it's been a joy to draw on everyone's personal stories, anecdotes and feelings around this destabilising period of life. What always feels miraculous about our work is how it transitions from the personal to the collective, much like a child finding their own feet and leading us in a direction we never could have imagined.

Stylistically, the show leans into what we love doing: ensemble-led, physical, humorous theatre, with heightened characters – full of silliness and heart.

We hope you recognise something of yourself – whether as a parent, a child, or somewhere in between. And we hope, for a moment, you can marvel at what it means to bring life into this strange, complicated, messy, beautiful world.

Helena Seneca, Jesse Jones,
May 2026

Characters

THE PARENTS
XANDER
MARGOT, *Xander's partner*
CELIA
DAVID, *Celia's partner*
BEA
KANE, *Bea's brother*
SIMONE
THE ENTERTAINER

THE CHILDREN
FELIX, *son of Xander and Margot*
AONGHUS, *son of Celia and David*
MAYA, *daughter of Bea and Jordan*
Other CHILDREN *at the parties*

Note on Performance

Our version of the play is set in Bristol, where many of us grew up. The text includes details relating to the city, and Bea's Bristolian accent is referenced in the play. If you are performing the show elsewhere, please feel free to adapt the location, details and accent to best serve your version of the play. The important thing is that it reflects the differences the characters feel exist between them.

For staging, we encourage you to lean away from the naturalistic and into the expressionist – the characters and the world are knowingly heightened.

For the WhatsApp section, the actors should embody the emojis.

This text went to press before the end of rehearsals and so may differ slightly from the play as performed.

Prelude

The red tabs of the theatre, onstage there is the ENTERTAINER*'s trunk of tricks.*

Some music hall-style music plays. An offstage voice on a microphone.

ENTERTAINER. Jellybabies and picklegerms, please put your hands together and raise the roof for the one, the only: the Magnificent Entertainer!

THE ENTERTAINER *enters wearing a white suit and top hat. He greets the crowd.*

You know, in my line of work you have to carry around a lot of stuff. A lot of baggage. My trusty old trunk is bursting at the seams and by golly it has been weighing me down! It's enough to make an old boy like me want to give up the ghost entirely.

But what's the Entertainer's remedy when your burden's weighing heavily?

That's right! Laughter is the best medicine, better-than-the-rest medicine.

Now let's see what we can do.

Folks, yesterday was a shocker. In the morning, I went to the opticians who tells me I'm colour-blind. Total shock, utter surprise – the news came out of the purple.

I get home at lunchtime, who do I find but a police officer waiting on my doorstep. 'Officer,' says I, 'what is the charge?' Officer says to me, 'Sir, I'm arresting you for stealing encyclopaedias.' 'Please, wait, officer,' I says, 'I can explain everything.'

In the evening, I go in for my limb-replacement surgery, but the surgeon bodged the job. I swear to god, if I ever find him, I'll kill him with my bear hands. Grr!

He pretends to make bear's hands.

Don't worry, kids, they're not really bear hands. Human hands, see? 'Tis but an illusion. I've always got a few Twix up me sleeve.

He pulls a Twix from his sleeve.

Who wants the Twix?

He offers the Twix to an audience member.

Hey, the other day I glued myself to my autobiography. That's my story and I'm sticking to it.

He throws the Twix to the audience member.

Knock knock.

Who's there?

Europe.

Europe who?

I am not a poo, grow up!

And last but not least, what do you call a man with no feet?

He kneels.

Neil.

That's right, folks! Welcome to my show, my world-famous show, hand-crafted with love and care to tantalise, hypnotise and mesmerise your old mince pies. But tonight is extra special, my lovelies, because tonight is my last show ever!

Can I get an 'aww'? Can I get an 'aah'? Can I get a 'what an absolute privilege it is to join you for your last ever show and we will miss you dearly'?

Close enough.

Now, hands up if you recognise me. Come on, don't be shy, hands up, every single one of you.

Of course you recognise me, my lovelies, because I recognise you. You are a crowd of ex-children. And I was there, wasn't I, at all of your little parties. Not a care in the cosmos to concern your coconuts.

Marvelled, you did. When I was blowing bubbles, playing tricks, turning long colourful balloons into dogs and cats and rabbits and bats. Making the ordinary, extraordinary.

He opens the trunk and is illuminated with light.

Magic! And it was magic, that time, wasn't it? Pure magic.

He shuts the trunk.

Give me a bloodcurdling howl if you wish you could go back!

He howls.
His hand goes to his chest.
His eyes go to his chest.
He stumbles.
He stumbles again.
He dies.
Pause.
Then he lifts his mic to his mouth.

Oh no. It seems I'm done for. I'm worm food. Looks like it's curtains for me.

The ENTERTAINER *waves his wand and the theatre tabs raise into the air, revealing a set covered in bright polka dots with five doors.*

Who will carry on my legacy? Who will take up the mantle? Someone?

Anyone? Son?

XANDER *appears onstage, in his underwear.*

You've not got your costume on! In there.

XANDER *gets his costume out from the trunk and gets dressed over the course of the following speech.*

Drum roll, please!

Transformation's the name of the game, folks. It happens to us all and it happens fast – quicker than a greyhound out the starting blocks. The most amazing trick ever pulled, rabies and diddlesquirms, is also the most common, for it is happening all. The. Time.

Hamlet becomes village becomes town becomes teeming metropolis. Babe becomes boy becomes teen becomes man. Man becomes 'dad'! Ta-dad!

Whizz, pop, bing-bang-boom, abracadabra alacazoom.

And now for my next trick!

THE ENTERTAINER *becomes a five-year-old boy,* FELIX.

PARTY ONE

XANDER *and* FELIX *are on a lovely street in Bristol.*

FELIX. It's Aonghus's party!

XANDER. I know.

FELIX. Then it's Maya's party.

XANDER. Yep.

FELIX. Then it's bedtime, then it's my party!

XANDER. I know, it's exciting, isn't it? Do you remember which house is theirs?

FELIX. No.

XANDER. Great, let me just call Mummy.

XANDER *gets his phone out and calls.*

MARGOT. All alright?

XANDER. Captain, I'm afraid to say, I am lost.

MARGOT. Good start. The address is on the invitation.

XANDER. Yes, that invitation is currently on our fridge.

MARGOT. Legend. Really excellent work.

XANDER. Okay good. Maybe you could just tell me what the house looks like?

MARGOT. Ummm, well, it's semi-detached. And it's like, nice. But not tacky or shouting about the fact that it's nice. It just *is* nice.

XANDER. This area used to be so rough – it's mad what twenty years and a couple of fancy bakeries does to a place.

XANDER *spots a banner.*

Wait, hang on, I've found a banner.

CELIA. 'Happy Birthday Aonghus, Five today, Our Superstar!'
'Party help, please go round the back.'

XANDER. Target located.

MARGOT. Great.

XANDER. Okay, okay. We'll be fine. I'll be fine. How are you
feeling?

MARGOT. I'm excited. Feels good to re-engage my PhD brain
but it's strange to be out in the world without my extra limb.

XANDER. Don't worry about Felix, he's going to have the best
party weekend ever! Right, monster?

FELIX. Yeah!

XANDER. You should be excited, you'll be great, everyone at
that conference is going to love you.

MARGOT. Yeah, I know.

XANDER. When are you back?

MARGOT. Six a.m. tomorrow. I should be there in time to set
things up for Felix's party.

But anything you can do today to get ahead would be really
useful.

XANDER. Yeah of course. I'll probably try and do most of it
today, to be fair.

MARGOT. Yep. Oh, and whatever you do. Do NOT let Celia
add you to the WhatsApp group.

XANDER. What WhatsApp group?

MARGOT. You'll see.

XANDER. Okay, Captain, I'm going in, wish me luck.

MARGOT. Luck. I promise you'll be fine.

XANDER. Love you, bye.

He hangs up.

Felix, what are you doing?

FELIX. I'm staring into the void!

XANDER. Not right now, mate.

FELIX. Daddy, did you know that Tommy Cooper died of a heart attack onstage?

XANDER. Yeah, I did, mate!

FELIX. How did Grandad die?

XANDER. He was very poorly, mate.

FELIX. Okay. Can I show you my magic trick, I've been practising.

XANDER. No, no, maybe later… Okay, Felix, listen now, mate, I need you to focus.

There are going to be a lot of people there today, a lot of kids and a lot of adults. So I need you to try and not be scared. I'd really like you to try and play along normally.

FELIX. Binky.

XANDER. I thought we were going to try without Binky today.

FELIX. I want Binky.

XANDER. Felix, come on please. Be a brave boy. Okay, here's Binky okay.

XANDER hands FELIX a hanky – his comfort object. XANDER takes a deep breath.

Alright, let's get this over with.

XANDER visibly puts on a front before ringing the doorbell. CELIA answers.

CELIA. Hello?

XANDER. Amazing to meet you. I'm Xander, Felix's dad.

CELIA. Ah, *the* Xander, we finally get to meet the mystery man himself, what a treat! Do come in, I'm just putting the finishing touches / to the party –

XANDER. Was it not nine-thirty?

CELIA. The invitation did say ten, but it's really not a bother.

XANDER. Ah, sorry. Margot told me it was nine-thirty.

CELIA. Not a bother at all, my lovelies. It's just you've caught me in set-up mode.

Haven't switched my personality on yet.

She presses an imaginary switch on her head and makes a powering-up noise.

There we are. Host Celia activated. Soo, Felix, have you come as a magician today?

XANDER. It's his latest thing. Maybe you should take the hat off now, mate?

CELIA. No, no, leave it on! It's lovely that you're expressing yourself.

DAVID jogs in in full running gear. Pants, then checks his smart watch.

DAVID. Yes! Yes, yes, yes, yes, yes, yes! Woo-hoo!

CELIA. David.

DAVID. Forty-one thirty-two for ten-point-six K. Do you know what that means, Celia? That puts me in the top two per cent for men of my age!

CELIA. We have guests.

DAVID. They're early.

CELIA. This is –

AONGHUS *bursts through the door.*

AONGHUS. I'm a Scallywag.

XANDER. Oh?

CELIA. Scallywags is a kids' modelling boutique. Our little looker's bagged himself an agent, haven't you, sweetheart?

DAVID. A real coup to get him on the ladder this early.

CELIA. Come on, Aonghus, show us your moneymaker.

AONGHUS *strikes a series of poses.* DAVID *and* CELIA *pretend to be photographers.*

You're gorgeous, you're marvellous, you're a modern-day Casanova.

XANDER. What do you say, Felix? Happy?

FELIX. Happy.

XANDER. Birthday.

FELIX. Birthday.

AONGHUS. Would you like to see my fashion show, Felix?

FELIX. Okay.

AONGHUS. Come on then.

AONGHUS *goes into the house.* FELIX *stays.*

XANDER. Go on then, Felix.

FELIX *hesitates.*

Felix, please, mate. For me?

FELIX *follows* AONGHUS *into the house.*

CELIA. Aw. You know, Felix is the most remarkable and sensitive boy.

DAVID. Mm.

CELIA. Aonghus is always telling me how much he admires and values him as a friend. Of course they do have their disagreements, but what little boys don't?

XANDER. I heard about the sports day debacle.

DAVID. Don't!

CELIA. So silly. Aonghus did win the sack race, it was a terrible call from Mrs Coles. That stupid bitch should have gone to Specsavers.

DAVID. Celia.

CELIA. Whoops.

CELIA *mimes zipping up her mouth, locking it and throwing away the key. She gestures to* DAVID *that she wants* DAVID *to unzip her mouth.* DAVID *finds the imaginary key and unzips her mouth; they laugh.*

DAVID. Here, let me take your jacket.

XANDER*'s jacket is removed by the* ENTERTAINER.

XANDER. No it's fine, I'll just wait a few minutes until he's settled.

DAVID. But we've only just managed to snare you. We're not going to let you get away that easily!

CELIA. Are you sure we can't lure you into the kitchen, just for a bit?

XANDER. I would love to, honestly –

DAVID. We've got…

BOTH. Perelló olives.

Pause.

XANDER. Well, why didn't you say so before?

DAVID. Marvellous! Marvellous!

XANDER*'s jacket reappears in front of* CELIA *and* DAVID.

Now, I'll take your jacket through to the back bedroom. Come this way!

They enter the house.

My beautiful wife Celia will take you through to the kitchen. Or Celia's Lair as I like to call it! Oh, and before I forget…

He produces a sticker that reads 'FELIX'S DAD' *and pats it onto* XANDER*'s chest.*

The finishing touch. Felix's dad.

Points to his own sticker.

Aonghus's daddy.

Points to CELIA*'s sticker.*

Aonghus's mummy.

CELIA. That's me!

DAVID. And you're the best mummy in the world.

CELIA. No, you are!

DAVID. No, I'm not a mummy, I'm a daddy!

They kiss. She sniffs.

CELIA. David, go shower, you dirty boy.

DAVID. I will. Just a sec. It's Wim Hof o'clock!

He leaves while taking deep Wim Hof-style breaths.

CELIA. I apologise. He gets overexcited. Follow me, lovely.

They start walking a complex route down the corridor.

So, Xander. Who are you? Who is Xander? What does Xander do?

XANDER. Well, Xander is a graphic designer…

CELIA. Really now? You know, the PTA could really use someone with your skills.

I'm the chair and I have big plans.

XANDER. I wish I could spare the time.

CELIA. Yes, you are a busy boy, aren't you! Never there for drop-off or pick-up or social events. Good thing you've got Margot.

XANDER. Yep, we're a good team.

CELIA. Of course you are. Xander, it is so lovely to finally meet you. I just can't believe it's taken us this long to connect.

XANDER. It's so good to connect.

CELIA. Well, consider us connected.

She holds on to both his hands.

Xander, I know it's been hard for you moving back home to Bristol after your father passed, I know it isn't the choice you would have made for yourself.

XANDER. How could you tell?

CELIA. I'm a very intuitive person. And also Margot told me. Even so, I can feel it emanating from you. And I want you to know that here you will find a new loving community, ready to embrace you.

XANDER. Thank you.

CELIA. With open arms.

XANDER. Thank you.

CELIA. Come here.

They hug.

XANDER. So how long have you been here?

CELIA. Two years, and we've only just scratched the surface. We love it.

Et voilà: la cuisine!

The ENTERTAINER *swoops in and points out objects in the kitchen.*

ENTERTAINER. Now isn't this nice!

A pastel-green Aga.

Floor-to-ceiling bookshelves.

A La Marzocco bean-to-cup espresso machine.

Kilner jars of dried organic pulses and grains. Wow.

XANDER. Wow.

CELIA. Now what can I get you to drink, lovely? We have elderflower and ginger, elderflower and rose, elderflower and pomegranate, just elderflower…

XANDER. Elderflower and ginger sounds lovely.

CELIA. Still or sparkling, lovely?

XANDER. Sparkling would be lovely.

CELIA. Lovely. Just a minute, the SodaStream's in the pantry.

XANDER. Still's fine if it's a bother.

CELIA. No bother.

XANDER. I don't want to be a bother.

CELIA. It's no bother, lovely.

She exits. A moment of XANDER *alone. His mask drops as he takes it all in.*

The ENTERTAINER, *dressed as a Victorian puppet-show master, enters.*

ENTERTAINER. Knock knock! Victor's Victorian Puppet Shows. Party for A-onghus?

XANDER. Celia!

ENTERTAINER. Don't worry, I'll find a corner. Nice pile of bricks, isn't it?

XANDER *is drawn to him.*

XANDER. Need any help?

ENTERTAINER. Nah. You're alright, mate.

The ENTERTAINER *leaves.* DAVID *enters with beers.*

DAVID. Beer?

XANDER. That was quick.

DAVID. I'm an efficient cleanser. Would you like a beer?

CELIA (*offstage*). He's having an elderflower and ginger!

DAVID. It's a birthday party! He can have two drinks if he wants. We've got non-alcoholic ones if you'd like?

XANDER. Great.

DAVID. This one is actually very special.

XANDER. Clear Head.

DAVID. Brewed locally, just down the road at the –

XANDER. – Bristol Beer Factory.

DAVID. Yes, that's right! I used to get a bit annoyed about

the price, until I found out they actually brew the beer with alcohol first / then remove the alcohol…

XANDER. Then take it out after –

DAVID. That's right! So in fact there are more steps to this than a normal beer.

XANDER. We should be paying more if anything!

DAVID. We should! You'll notice it says on the side 'This Beer Saves Lives'. That's because they donate a portion of their earnings to a men's mental health charity. Isn't that great?

XANDER. That's brilliant.

DAVID. To men's mental health.

XANDER. To men's mental health.

CELIA *returns.*

CELIA. Ice?

XANDER. Please, just a little bit. Oh, here's a little something for the birthday boy. It's one of those plastic dinosaur-egg thingies.

CELIA. Ah.

XANDER. Is that okay?

CELIA. That's fine, that's absolutely fine! The invite did say no presents.

XANDER. Oh, sorry.

CELIA. We just don't want a house full of tat. We really appreciate the thought though. I'll just pop it on the table over there.

She chucks the present – the ENTERTAINER *catches it in his hat.* CELIA *notices him.*

Can we just discuss content warnings re: the puppet show, is there any mild peril?

CELIA *exits.*

DAVID. So you moved down from London?

XANDER. Yep.

DAVID. Same!

XANDER. Whereabouts?

DAVID. Crouch End, born and raised. Yourself?

XANDER. Hackney.

DAVID. I like your teeny beanie.

XANDER. I love your cords.

DAVID. I cannot believe it's been a whole year since our kids started school together and we're only just meeting. Have you been avoiding us?

XANDER. No, no, I had a big design job with a client and I've been working on my dad's house.

DAVID. No need to explain yourself, Xander. I'd avoid us too if I were you. But I'm glad we've got you now. And there's no escape.

CELIA *re-enters.*

CELIA. Heather?

DAVID. That's not Heather, that's Xander!

CELIA. Idiot. Would you like a sprig of heather in your elderflower, Xander?

DAVID. It's from the garden.

XANDER. A sprig of heather, whatever the weather – yes please.

CELIA. That's a yes to the heather!

She leaves.

DAVID. Oh, and Xander. Don't join the WhatsApp group.

CELIA *re-enters with drinks.*

CELIA. I took the liberty of popping a straw in there for you. It's paper, so when you're finished just pop it out, and pop it in the recycling.

XANDER. That's fine. I'll just pop it in here. (*Puts the straw in his mouth.*) Cheers, guys. To the weekend of many parties!

ALL. To the weekend of many parties!

They cheers.

CELIA. David, let's refresh ourselves re: schedule.

XANDER. Schedule?

CELIA. Yes. Ten a.m. we'll break the ice with hook-a-ducky.

DAVID. Ten-fifteen – treasure hunt.

CELIA. Big prizes to be won.

DAVID. Ten-thirty – make your own pizza.

CELIA. It's not pizza. It's flatbread. It's sourdough flatbread.

DAVID. Ten-fifty-five – pass the parcel.

CELIA. I stayed up till midnight wrapping all the layers.

DAVID. Eleven-ten – elevenses.

CELIA. We've got the most delicious catering from the little tapas place round the corner.

DAVID. With some home-made additions.

CELIA. David's smoked salmon mini bagel bites.

DAVID. Patent pending. Eleven-twenty – Victorian puppet show!

CELIA. Eleven-thirty – musical statues!

DAVID. Eleven-forty-five – the cake.

CELIA. Twelve o'clock…

DAVID/CELIA. Party bags! The best birthday party EVER!

They rub their noses together. The doorbell rings.

CELIA. Ah, the first guests have arrived. The ones who can read the invitation properly at least, haha! Kidding, I'm kidding!

She heads for the door.

Oh and Xander, I wanted to mention that some of us loony parents are on a WhatsApp group. We call ourselves 'The

Elite Mummies (and Daddies) Club'. So silly, really. Remind me to add you.

She leaves.

DAVID. Don't do it.

CELIA (*offstage*). David, the labels!

DAVID (*to* CELIA). Yes, my love! (*To* XANDER.) Duty calls.

He leaves.

SIMONE *appears,* XANDER *jumps out of his skin. She has hair over her face like the girl in* The Ring. *She is holding a baby. The sound of wind.*

Pause.

XANDER. Hello?

DAVID *and* CELIA *re-enter.*

CELIA. Ah! You've met Simone, Dante's mum! Simone's just had her second. We have her round all the time. It takes a village. Particularly with a new baby. But she's doing so well. SO WELL!

DAVID. Hiya Simone. How is the best mummy ever?! Isn't it the most magical time?

CELIA. Are you cherishing every minute?

DAVID. How's your little miracle?

CELIA. Did you read the articles we sent you?

DAVID. The transformative power of yak's milk?

CELIA. Parent–baby breath alignment?

DAVID. One up two down?

CELIA. Lunar sleep cycle?

Silence.

DAVID *and* CELIA *laugh.*

DAVID. Simone! You are brilliant!

SIMONE *exits.*

God. She's the best.

AONGHUS *arrives in the doorway.*

AONGHUS. EVERYONE LOOK AT ME, IT'S MY PARTY!

An orchestral version of 'Soda Pop' from KPop Demon Hunters *plays. Children, wearing animal masks, flood the stage for a montage of Aonghus's party, all presided over by* CELIA. FELIX *plays alone. At the end of the sequence,* BEA *arrives.*

BEA. Sorry I'm late.

CELIA. Bea!

XANDER *clocks her then hides in a cupboard.*

BEA. Oh my god, this renovation!

CELIA. I know.

BEA. This is –

CELIA. I know.

BEA. Where did you –

CELIA. My sister's an interior designer.

BEA. Jesus. That's just…

CELIA. I know.

BEA. You have an Aga.

CELIA. You don't have to tell me, I already know. Oh Bea, lovely, David over-catered, he made three hundred mini bagel bites, they may be mini but there are *three hundred* of them, if you could take a few home for Maya's party you'd be doing us a real favour.

BEA. I've already got loads of food, babes.

CELIA. Never mind. Oh, it's time for the puppet show! À bientôt!

CELIA *leaves.*

DAVID. Did you need something from the pantry, Xander?

　XANDER *steps out.*

XANDER. Hi, Bea.

BEA. Oh. Hi. Alex.

DAVID. Have you two met?

XANDER. No –

BEA. – Yes

XANDER. I mean, yes. Yeah we have, yeah.

BEA. We were at school together.

DAVID. You weren't!

BEA. We were. Alex and I have known each other since we were little kids.

XANDER. It's Xander now.

BEA. Ooh, lah-di-dah. Xander. That's nice.

DAVID. Wow. You must have some stories to tell.

XANDER. Ah, no we don't.

DAVID (*shouting*). Celia! Get this!

CELIA (*shouting offstage*). What?

DAVID. Bea and Xander went to school together!

CELIA (*shouting offstage*). No! Really? That's amazing.

BEA. I haven't seen you for years.

DAVID (*shouting*). They haven't seen each other for years!

CELIA (*shouting offstage*). Wow! I can't believe that! They must have some stories to tell.

BEA (*reading his name tag*). Felix's dad. So you're Margot's partner?! Margot and Alex? Well done you!

XANDER. Haha. What do you mean?

BEA. Got a trendy new wardrobe too, I see. Been hitting the gym as well?

Typical; goes to London, has a kid, gets a teeny beanie and a six-pack.

Meanwhile muggins over here gets postpartum depression and mastitis.

XANDER. I had the hat before the kid.

BEA. I'm joking! A little joke.

XANDER. Haha.

BEA. Your kid's party's tomorrow, right? Snap! Mine's this afternoon. Look at us, with our summer babies! A couple of proper adults now.

DAVID (*mimicking* BEA*'s accent*). 'Proper'! Delightful.

BEA (*to* XANDER). Where's your accent gone?

The ENTERTAINER *enters for his puppet show.*

ENTERTAINER. Gather round, kids!

XANDER. Um. It hasn't.

ENTERTAINER. Once upon a time there was a little boy who lived in a town with his loving father in a tiny little house no bigger than a shoebox.

And oh, how simple and sweet was life. Not a care in the cosmos to concern their coconuts.

And as he grew older, he found himself a-courting with his next-door neighbour, the daughter of his father's oldest friend, and the most beautiful young maiden in all the land.

'I fancy you.' 'I fancy you too.' 'Mwah.'

And all things and all people were in their right place. And everything seemed to make sense.

But one night, as the boy slept, the Devil appeared outside his window.

Tap tap tap.

'Little boy, little boy, let me come in.'
'Not by the hair on my chinny-chin-chin!'

'Very well,' said the Devil, 'I'll speak from the cold.
You are young, you are handsome, you are noble and bold.
Where do you wish that you will grow old?'

'Why, here,' said the boy.
The Devil guffawed.
'You could grow old here, but you'd grow mighty bored.
Look out of the window, what do you spy?'

'I see the glittering lights of the sky.'
'Those stars could be yours, if only you'd try.'

DAVID. So were the two of you close?

XANDER/BEA. Um… yeah.

DAVID. Bea, how rude of me – can I get you something
to drink?

BEA. Oh. I don't know. Um.

XANDER. You'll like the elderflower and ginger.

BEA. Will I?

DAVID. One elderflower and ginger, coming right up.

BEA. Thank you.

DAVID *exits. There is a long awkward silence before* CELIA
runs in.

CELIA. Technology emergency. Alexa is not responding, that
puppet show was so weird, and I've just found out one of the
children is allergic to sesame, so that's the hummus in the
compost. Can one of you DJ for musical statues? Someone
who has Bluetooth.

XANDER. Eeer, I can.

CELIA. Thanks so much, Xander, you superstar. Time for
musical statues with DJ Felix's dad! Kids!!

The kids run in.

XANDER *plays 'Wind the Bobbin Up'. The children dance.
He stops the music.*

Okay, Frank, Afeni, Merryn, Remi, bad luck you're losers! Come and get a dried apricot.

He plays 'The Wheels on the Bus'. He stops it. AONGHUS *sneakily pushes* MAYA.

Oooh sorry, Maya, out you come!

XANDER. Hey, Aonghus…

CELIA. Is still in, yep.

XANDER. Maya, are you okay?

CELIA. Maestro!

XANDER. Huh?

CELIA. I said Maestro!

AONGHUS. I want better music.

XANDER. What's wrong with the music?

AONGHUS. It's for babies!

XANDER. What do you mean it's for babies, it's just… Fine, fine. I'll change it.

XANDER *struggles with his phone.*

CELIA. What's going on?

XANDER. Nothing, just having some connection issues.

DAVID. Need a hand with your baby music?

XANDER. No, I don't need a hand, I just need this to work. Please work, why won't you work?

AONGHUS. Felix's dad sucks.

AONGHUS *kicks* XANDER *in the shin. It really hurts but he pretends it doesn't.*

DAVID. Haha! Oh dear, Aonghy, gentle toes, please – welcome to party season, eh Xander?

XANDER *plays 'Angel' by Massive Attack. The kids dance in their animal masks.* XANDER *zooms out on his life. He is mortified.*

He stops the music.

XANDER. Right, Aonghus, sorry, mate, but you're still dancing there. Out you come. Felix is the winner!

CELIA. No, he wasn't.

XANDER. Sorry?

CELIA. He was frozen.

XANDER. No, he's still doing this with his arms.

He demonstrates AONGHUS*'s arm movement.*

CELIA. He's perfectly still. He was frozen. And it's his special day. Yes?

XANDER. Yes.

Stand-off.

CELIA. Aonghy is the winner!

CELIA, DAVID *and* AONGHUS *share a family cuddle.*

XANDER. I – Excuse me, he wasn't…

BEA. Just leave it.

CELIA. Aww, thanks for that. Superstar!

DAVID. Some interesting song choices there, DJ. Hey, maybe don't give up the day job.

XANDER. Thanks, David, I wasn't planning on it.

DAVID. Good.

The lights cut. SIMONE *appears upstage with a cake. She hums 'Happy Birthday'.* AONGHUS *blows out the candles.* SIMONE *disappears.*

DAVID. Classic Simone.

CELIA. Now wasn't that the best party ever! Hemp party bags through here.

They're biodegradable! Over to yours now, Bea!

BEA. Okay, showtime. Let's do this!

BEA *leaves.* FELIX *burrows his head into* XANDER.

XANDER. David, are you still happy to take my Felix over to Bea's?

DAVID. Of course. Plenty of room in the Elgrand. You're not joining us?

XANDER. No. I've got to get back to set up for Felix's party.

CELIA. Oh, that's a shame! We've only just started getting to know you properly.

XANDER. Such a shame. Okay, Felix. You're going to go with David and Aonghy now, okay?

FELIX. I don't want to go.

AONGHUS. What's wrong with him, Daddy?

DAVID. Nothing's wrong with him, he's just a bit of a sensitive boy, that's all.

FELIX *starts to cry.*

XANDER. Please don't cry, mate. Please stop crying.

FELIX. Can't we go home?

XANDER. No, Felix. You've got a whole other party to go to. Isn't that fun? More friends!

FELIX. Don't leave me.

XANDER *takes a deep breath.*

XANDER. Don't worry. Daddy's here. I'll come. Okay?

FELIX. Okay.

XANDER. Go and grab your party bag!

FELIX *runs off.*

DAVID. Bless his little cotton socks.

CELIA. You are doing such a good job, Daddy.

AONGHUS. No, you're not.

CELIA. Oh and Xander, I hope you don't mind. I took the liberty of adding you to the WhatsApp group. Welcome to the club!

They all leave. XANDER falls to the floor and nurses his sore shin. The ENTERTAINER comes in and puts a plaster on it before resuming his act.

ENTERTAINER. How we doing, folks? Still with us? Just a quick one for you: the other day I bought some coconut shampoo, but when I got home I realised I don't even own a coconut!

Drum sting.

Now we're off, I thought it would be a good idea for you to get to know me better. As you already know my name is 'Entertainer'. But what you may not know is that that is, in fact, my real name. N Tertainer. N being short for Neil. Neil Tertainer, my name is Neil Tertainer. It's the name on my birth certificate!

If you were from where I'm from, you'd be familiar with the Tertainer family. We're one of those clans that are locked to their locale, we're part of the furniture. A long line of entertainers. My old man and his old man and his old man and fifteen old men before that, all made their way in this world through spit and sawdust, singing silly songs, spinning plates and sleight of hand.

XANDER. Can you stop showing off?

ENTERTAINER (*to audience*). Just a moment. (*To XANDER.*) Would you like some battered cod?

XANDER. What?

ENTERTAINER. To go with that great big chip on your shoulder!

XANDER. Everyone's laughing at you!

ENTERTAINER. Of course they are! That's the point!

The ENTERTAINER becomes FELIX, being carried on XANDER's back.

MARGOT. What did you just say?

XANDER. Nothing.

MARGOT. Their house is incredible isn't it? I keep badgering Celia to pass on her sister's number – she's an interior designer.

XANDER. Yeah, I heard. How's it all going on the other side of the channel?

MARGOT. To be honest I had a nightmare with the hotel booking, the room wasn't up to scratch so I got them to swap me to another but the view is of a horrible little back alley.

XANDER. Oh dear.

MARGOT. Yeah, it's really not on.

FELIX. Hi, Mummy!

MARGOT. Hi monster, how's your magic going?

FELIX. I can nearly make myself disappear.

MARGOT. Wow.

XANDER. Are you ready for your big presentation?

MARGOT. Yeah, I'm feeling good about it. How are you doing? Is Felix having fun?

XANDER. Yeah, it's great, he is grand. Nothing to worry about on our end.

MARGOT. Aw yay, well done you two! Did you meet Bea?

XANDER. Yep.

MARGOT. She's sweet, isn't she?

XANDER. I dunno. Barely spoke to her.

MARGOT. Well, you'll love her.

PARTY TWO

*'APT' by Bruno Mars and Rosé plays. A group of children flood
the stage. They do a choreographed dance.*

ENTERTAINER. Another house, similar in structure but very
different in character. Same bones, different clothes.

The kids all run around, amped up on the party atmosphere.

BEA. Welcome to the madhouse! Alright, kids!

She gets everything under control.

Hands on your heads! Hands on your shoulders! Hands on
your knees! Shoulders! Knees! Toes! Lips!

And shhhh.

Now listen to me, everyone, it's very important. So today is
Maya's birthday and Maya is one hundred years old.

MAYA. No, I'm not!

BEA. Yes, she is. She's one hundred years old.

KIDS (*ad-libbed*). No, she's not! / She's a thousand! / She's
a million! (*Etc.*)

BEA. Okay, you're right, she's actually five… hundred years old.

KIDS (*ad-libbed*). One zillion billion! / She's a baby! / She's so
old! (*Etc.*)

BEA. Uh, excuse me!

KIDS. Shhhhh.

BEA. Now I need you all to make me one promise, can you do
that?

KIDS. Ye–

BEA. Uh!

The kids nod.

Because this is *my* house, I make the rules. And I have one rule that is so important for you all to follow. And that rule is… have the most fun ever!!!

The kids go absolutely ballistic. They run into the garden.

CELIA *and* DAVID *applaud her.*

CELIA. She's a natural!

DAVID. I have no idea how you do that!

CELIA. You make it look so easy.

BEA. Show no fear. Rule number one. Okay, we've got Pom Bears, Pringles, Party Rings, Quavers.

DAVID (*mimicking* BEA*'s accent*). Quavers!

BEA. Yes, David, Quavers. And fish fritters!

CELIA. None for Aonghy, please! Fried food agitates his gut microbiome.

XANDER *and the* ENTERTAINER *enter.* XANDER *scans the kitchen.*

ENTERTAINER. A nostalgic scene.
A Royal Doulton Princess Diana mug.
A collection of masks from across the world.
A framed oil painting of Black Jesus.
A familiar smell – Britney Spears's Midnight Fantasy perfume.
A vintage poster from Jamaica that reads, 'When you come here –

XANDER. 'What you see here –

ENTERTAINER. 'What you hear here –

XANDER. 'When you leave here –

ENTERTAINER. 'Let it stay here –

BOTH. 'Or don't come back here.'

ENTERTAINER. And there. There on the fridge, held with a magnet…

XANDER *almost reaches towards it.*

CELIA, DAVID *and* BEA *notice* XANDER.

DAVID. Whatcha looking at, X-man?

BEA. Now that is a photo of my seventh birthday party.

CELIA. Big crowd! Someone's popular.

BEA. Mostly aunties. That's me in the middle.

DAVID. I can see that.

CELIA. Who's holding your hand there?

XANDER. That's me.

CELIA/DAVID. Nooo!!!

BEA. Cute, right?

CELIA. It's so nice that you two are reconnecting.

DAVID. Who's the man in the flamboyant suit?

BEA. That's Xander's dad.

DAVID. No!

BEA. He was an entertainer, wasn't he, Xander?

XANDER. It was just a side thing, it wasn't…

CELIA. He looks like a real character.

XANDER. He was just a plasterer.

BEA. He was a local legend. Did all the kids' birthday parties around here. What was the name of his act again, Xand?

XANDER. I don't remember.

BEA. Of course you do, you were his little assistant.

XANDER. Only sometimes.

BEA. The Magnificent Neil Tertainer!

CELIA *and* DAVID *laugh uproariously.*

XANDER. It was embarrassing.

A beat.

You've got loads of stuff from your parents' house.

BEA. Yeah, reminds me of who I am.

CELIA. I love a vintage feel. Heirlooms just hold a deeper
significance, I find.

BEA. You know what, Celia? I agree.

CELIA. Bea, thank you so much for opening your home to us.

BEA. To be honest, mate, it's my absolute worst nightmare
having people in my house.

DAVID. So, Bea, where's Maya's daddy?

BEA. He works weekends.

CELIA/DAVID. Awwwww.

CELIA. Xander, you've got to meet Maya's daddy.

BEA. His name's Jordan. Calling him Daddy freaks me out.

XANDER. Jordan? Jordan Deacon?

BEA. Yeah.

DAVID. And he is a top daddy!

XANDER. I'm sure he is.

The ENTERTAINER, *dressed as a modern DJ, enters, his
trunk now contains disco lights.*

DJ. DJ for Maya?

BEA. In the garden.

DJ. Great.

CELIA/DAVID. So. What's the schedule?

BEA. No schedule, the DJ will keep them entertained. Right,
help yourself to drinks, we've got squash, fizzy drinks, cider.

CELIA. Bea, lovely. Aonghus is drinking something. It looks
fluorescent.

BEA. It's a Panda Pop.

CELIA. What is that?

BEA. It's a drink, Celia.

The DJ *throws her a Panda Pop.*

CELIA. HAHAHAHA! Yeah completely totally yeah. I'm juussst reading the ingredients and there's quuuuuite a lot of Es on here. It feels a lickle bit like it's screaming at me. EEEEEEEE!

BEA. Yeah, I had to buy them in bulk. Pretty sure they might be illegal now.

CELIA. Hahahahaha. We're just kind of a no-sugar household / and I just saw Aonghus neck three.

MAYA *and* AONGHUS *run through laughing. They are throwing snap bangs on the floor.*

AONGHUS. War! Waaaaaar!!!

CELIA. Careful please! Always at the floor, never at the face!

BEA. Oooooh they'll be fine!

CELIA. I could run some games with the little ones? Pass the… pass the Pringles?

BEA. They're happy running about outside.

CELIA. I think they could benefit from a little structure.

BEA. Look, as long as they're not downing bleach or chuffing on vapes then they can be as unstructured as they want.

DAVID (*looking into the garden*). They do now seem to be getting quite feral.

BEA. Eat dirt, get hurt. That's the order of the afternoon. Cider, Xander? Is that still your tipple of choice?

XANDER. Oh, not for me, thanks.

DAVID. He's more of a craft beer guy, aren't you, Xand?

BEA. We don't have any of those. Sorry.

DJ. Big up the birthday girl. Happy birthday, Maya. Five years old today – you don't look a day over four. This one goes out to you.

Everyone dances to 'Gangnam Style' by PSY. Suddenly it cuts back to…

XANDER. So, are your parents…?

BEA. Still about, yeah. Same house, just round the corner. It made sense to be close to them.

XANDER. This is lovely. You've got a nice house.

BEA. Thank you, Xander.

XANDER. Really nice.

BEA. Are you surprised?

XANDER. No.

BEA. What were you expecting?

XANDER. I dunno.

BEA. A tiny little shoebox?

XANDER. No.

BEA. A home for tiny mice? Little small Bea in her little small home?

XANDER. No.

BEA (*she does an exaggerated Bristolian accent*). Alright Xand, alright maaaate, yerrr welcome to my 'ouse. It ain't much but it's mine. Somewhere to stash me cheese at least.

CELIA/DAVID. Haha.

XANDER. I didn't mean anything by it. It was a compliment.

BEA. I have done well, to be fair, got a job straight out of school, rose up the ranks, started my own agency, had the kids, and now here we are…

XANDER. Good for you.

BEA. I love it.

XANDER. What?

BEA. This. All of it.

MAYA (*offstage*). Muuuuum?

BEA. Yes, love?

MAYA (*offstage*). Can you wipe my bum?

BEA. Remember you can do it yourself, love.

MAYA (*offstage*). Oh, yeeeaaah.

BEA. My life, I love it.

XANDER. Great.

BEA. Okay. This is good. We're good. Everything's good.

The ENTERTAINER *rewinds the decks.*

DJ. Rewwiiinnd.

KANE *enters, sunglasses on, looking cool as hell. Everyone looks at him.*

KANE. I heard there was a party.

BEA. Kane?!

KANE. But this looks more like a waiting room, and not for something good. Oi, DJ, chuck us a kombucha.

DJ *throws* KANE *a kombucha.*

BEA. I didn't know you were coming.

KANE. You did invite me.

BEA. I didn't even know you were in the country.

KANE. I wouldn't miss my nephew's birthday!

BEA. Niece.

KANE. I wouldn't miss my niece's birthday!

DAVID. Sorry, excuse me, whose daddy are you?

KANE. No one's daddy.

Hey, DJ, give us the mic.

Allow me.

KANE *walks downstage into a spotlight. Throughout the following monologue, the parents gradually melt in envy.*

Let me lay out my typical Saturday for you.

Get up at half-nine.

ENSEMBLE. Half-nine!

KANE. Maybe ten.

ENSEMBLE. Ten!

KANE. Maybe even eleven.

ENSEMBLE. Nooooo.

KANE. Just whenever I naturally wake up, really, when my body is ready and rested.

Head into town, have a coffee, read the paper. Or stay in bed and watch Netflix. It's up to me.

ENSEMBLE. It's up to him!

KANE. I decide. Then I'll go for a run. Or not, if I don't feel like it. It's up to me.

ENSEMBLE. It's up to him!

KANE. Make some lunch and eat it in peace and quiet.

ENSEMBLE. Peace and quiet!

KANE. Maybe I'll have a beer, maybe I won't, I will check in and see how I feel.

And then I've got the whole afternoon to myself. I can read, or journal, or swim, or work out, or have a long, hot bath, uninterrupted.

ENSEMBLE. Uninterrupted!

KANE. Or have a really long nap, or call my mum – have a good ol' natter.

And then maybe in the evening I'll go out to a restaurant, or link up with mates and get really, really, really drunk. Find a hot girl or a hot guy.

BEA. Or both!

KANE. Go back to theirs, and spend the whole night making love.

ENSEMBLE. The whooole night?

KANE. Wake up, go home and do it all again. It's. Up. To. Me.

ENSEMBLE. It's up to him!

KANE (*bigger*). It's. Up. To. Me!

ENSEMBLE. It's up to him!

KANE (*even bigger*). IT'S. UP. TO. MEEE.

> *We snap back to reality, everyone pretends not to be envious*

ENSEMBLE. That does sound quite pleasant actually. / Interesting. / Sounds great. (*Etc.*)

KANE. Nice to meet you all, I'm Bea's brother.

CELIA. I'm Celia, chair of the PTA.

KANE. Okay.

DAVID. I'm David, husband of the chair of the PTA.

BEA. Where have you flown in from this time then?

KANE. Sri Lanka.

DAVID. Sri Lanka! I've travelled there a couple of times myself with work. Mainly seen the inside of hotel rooms but beautiful country, beautiful food.

KANE. Beautiful country, beautiful food, beautiful people. Talking of beautiful people, Bea, my favourite sister, I'm going to need somewhere to crash.

BEA. Fucksake.

> MAYA *enters.*

MAYA. Uncle Kane!

KANE. Now where is my favourite niecey-boo?

MAYA. I'm here!

KANE. That can't be Maya.

MAYA. It is!

KANE. That's a full-grown adult person!

MAYA. No, I'm not. I am a child. Have you got me a present?

KANE. Uh yeah. I got you… this half a packet of chewing gum. Aaaaand, this little bottle of magic potion.

He pulls out a mini bottle of airplane gin, he quickly drinks it then gives it to MAYA.

BEA. Kane, seriously?

Pause.

MAYA. This is the best present ever! Look, Mummy, I'm a giant!!

She runs off.

KANE. You're welcome!

As MAYA *runs for the door,* KANE *notices* XANDER.

Alex?!

XANDER. Alright, Kane. Good to see you.

KANE. What are you doing here?!

CELIA. Oh you two know each other too!?

DAVID. Delightful.

KANE. This is wild! It feels like Mercury retrograde in Pisces on a full moon. The past can be so activating.

XANDER. I didn't mean to activate you, mate.

KANE. I can't imagine *she* was best pleased to see you.

BEA. She has a name.

CELIA. Oh do spill, is there gossip?

KANE. No gossip, just truth.

XANDER. There's nothing to say.

CELIA. Oh come on, we're all friends here.

XANDER. No, we're not.

CELIA. Sorry?

KANE. The truth will always come to light so let's call out the tension!

BEA. Can I just remind everyone that this is a five-year-old's birthday party, not an episode of *Jeremy Kyle*?

DAVID. Is that a television programme?

CELIA. Yes, one of those ones that's on in the daytime.

XANDER. There's no tension. Everything is fine. We're all having a really good time!

DJ. Kids, it's now time to send this party from ordinary to extraordinary. Right now, you are the youngest you will ever be. So grab this moment with both hands. Let's go!

The DJ *plays 'Sandstorm' by Darude. The* DJ *really dances.*

Slide on your knees.
Hide behind the curtain.
Hug your mummy's leg.
Hold your best friend's hand.
Hold your enemy's hand.
Your enemy is now your best friend too.
Soon you will have mortgages.
Soon you will have lifetime ISAs.
Soon you will have to put stupid petrol in your stupid car.
But for now, there is only possibility. Infinite possibility.

Snap back to the kitchen.

KANE. So are we really not going to talk about what happened between you two?

BEA. Dude, it's my kid's birthday party, it's not the time to unpack all that baggage.

XANDER. Baggage?

KANE. Our children's parties can really bring up memories from our primary and secondary socialisation.

BEA. How would you know, you don't have kids?!

KANE. I am an empath. And I just feel that Alex has some explaining to do.

XANDER. Maybe we could do this without an audience?

DAVID. Oh, we can leave if you'd like.

CELIA. Aonghus just vomited!!

BEA. What?

DAVID. Oh dear.

CELIA. He's overstimulated. He gets very anxious when there's no structure, Bea.

We really need some activities!

BEA. Okay, what do you want to do?!

CELIA. Can't we all just play some nice quiet calm games.

DJ. Did someone say games? Tug o' War!

The kids go wild.

KIDS. Tug of War!

CELIA. Oh no no no.

DAVID. Oh fun!

CELIA. Could we call it something more cooperative? Like Tug of Peace?

DJ. What we need now is two brave, bold leaders.

MAYA. That's me!

DAVID. And birthday boy Aonghus of course!

DJ. Now it's time to pick! Your! Teams!

MAYA. Hannah.

AONGHUS. George.

MAYA. Lily.

AONGHUS. Dante.

MAYA. Maelle

AONGHUS. Cooper.

MAYA. Poppy.

AONGHUS. That's it.

MAYA. My team is going to destroy your team.

AONGHUS. Your team is dead meat.

DAVID. Ha! That's my boy.

XANDER. Hang on, what about Felix?

DAVID. Go on, Aonghus, pick Felix.

AONGHUS. I don't want to.

XANDER. Well, you're going to have to –

CELIA. We can't make him.

XANDER. What, yes you can.

FELIX. Daddy, I don't need to play.

　　AONGHUS *transitions to* KANE.

KANE. I know this party is 'for the kids', but, Bea, it's your 'birthing' day too and you're not having fun. No one is having fun.

DAVID. I'm having fun.

BEA. Kane, behave yourself, you absolute child.

　　KANE *transitions back to* AONGHUS.

MAYA. I'm ready to play now. My team is getting bored.

DAVID. Yes, shall we just start the game?

XANDER. It's Aonghus's turn, so he should pick Felix! You're not being very nice, Aonghus.

CELIA. What is this? A character assassination?!

XANDER. Just pick him, mate. Just pop him on your team, lovely.

　　COME ON, MATE.

You're obviously hurting his feelings, so…

All eyes on FELIX.

FELIX. Daddy, I don't even want to play!

XANDER. Yes, you do. Come on, Felix.

AONGHUS. No! It's MY BIRTHDAY. I don't want Felix on my team.

AONGHUS *transitions to* KANE.

BEA. This isn't the place.

KANE. Bea, I don't know why you're running away from the past.

MAYA. Mummy, why are you running away from the past?

BEA. I'm not. I'm not running away from anything. Everything is fine.

XANDER. Everything is fine!

KANE. Your aura is literally on fire.

XANDER. My aura is FINE. Can you just leave me alone?!

KANE *transforms to* AONGHUS.

Fine, Aonghus, we don't want to go on your team. We'll go on the girls' team!! Yay!

MAYA. Nooo.

XANDER. Okay. Let's go! Three, two, one!

XANDER *pulls the rope hard, causing* AONGHUS *to fall to the ground.*

A beat.

AONGHUS *howls.*

CELIA. Aonghus!! Everyone back away NOW.

CELIA *turns into a dragon and breathes fire. Everyone runs away.*

Are you hurt, my sweet one? Are you hurt? It's okay. I'm here. Mummy's right here. Oh my gosh, are you okay? Let me have a look. Where is it hurting? CAN SOMEONE GET A FLANNEL! I need ICE! A cold compress! Arnica cream, stat!

AONGHUS. That man hurt me!

CELIA. It was awful. You're okay now. I'll make it better.

> FELIX *offers* CELIA *Binky.*

Get that disgusting rag away from me.

> CELIA *sets Binky on fire with her dragon breath.*

BEA. Is everyone else okay?

KIDS. Yeah.

BEA. Great, down at the end of this hall is a very special room, the cinema room! And *Encanto* is ready to play! Go go go!

> AONGHUS *suddenly feels fine, he leaps up as all the kids exit.*

AONGHUS. We don't talk about Brunoooo!

It is just the parents left.

CELIA. You should be ashamed of yourself, young man. Am I the only person here with a sense of responsibility?!

XANDER. It was an accident.

CELIA. Do you have something you want to say to Aonghus?

XANDER. I – er.

DAVID. She means sorry.

XANDER. Yeah, I know. Sorry.

CELIA. What was that?

XANDER. SORRY, AONGHUS.

CELIA. Good. We forgive you. Now, Xander, whilst I've got you here, the PTA are raising funds for a new frog bin in the playground.

XANDER. Sorry?

CELIA. A frog bin. You know…

She does an impression of a frog bin.

Can we count on your support?

XANDER. Yes.

CELIA. Quite right.

A beat.

I'm going to see if Aonghus is concussed.

DAVID. And I'm going to find some Calpol.

They leave.

XANDER. I want to go home.

BEA. What did you say?

XANDER. I think Felix is probably going to want to leave.
Felix!

FELIX. What?

XANDER. We've got to go now.

FELIX. I want to stay.

XANDER. You can't, monster, we've got to get back to –

FELIX. I want to stay and watch *Encanto.*

XANDER. I know, mate, but we've got to set up for your party,
remember.

FELIX. You embarrassed me. You shouted and then you hurt
Aonghy and you made Celia breathe fire. You embarrassed
me in front of all my friends.

XANDER. Embarrassing? You're embarrassing.

FELIX. I want Mummy.

XANDER. I'm sorry, mate. I didn't mean that.

The adults watch FELIX leave.

Felix, you dropped Binky.

The past intrudes. FELIX *becomes* ENTERTAINER, *who becomes Dad.*

ENTERTAINER. Knock knock.

XANDER. Not now.

ENTERTAINER. What's gotten into you lately, mate?

XANDER. Nothing.

ENTERTAINER. You just seem irritable. You're like a man with a fork in a world full of soup.

XANDER. Everything's always a joke with you, isn't it?

ENTERTAINER. No.

XANDER. All a big performance.

ENTERTAINER. Now come on, that's not fair.

XANDER. Don't worry, come September I'll be off and you can get on with your stupid little act in peace.

ENTERTAINER. Al –

XANDER. Get out of my room.

ENTERTAINER. Okay.

XANDER. Get out of my room!

ENTERTAINER. I'm going.

The ENTERTAINER *leaves.*

KANE. And then there were three.

BEA. Kane. He's not okay.

XANDER *goes for one of the doors, it closes.*

KANE. No, clearly, why were you so mental with that annoying kid who looks like a model?

XANDER. I need to check on Felix.

He goes for another door, it closes.

KANE. I just want to hear your side of the story.

XANDER. He was being a twat.

KANE. Our story.

XANDER. What do you want me to say?

KANE. I want to know why you ghosted us.

XANDER. I went to university and we drifted apart. It happens.

He goes for another door. Closes.

KANE. Yes people drift apart, but you completely disappeared.

XANDER. I don't know.

Another door. He can't escape.

KANE. Fifteen years is a long time… You stopped coming home, you stopped answering our calls. Bea didn't know whether you were still in a relationship.

BEA. It's okay, I'm okay. I wasn't but I am now.

KANE. We deserve to know why.

XANDER. I don't know how to explain it.

MAYA (*offstage*). Muuuuuuum.

KANE. Explain what?

BEA. Yes, love?

XANDER. You wouldn't get it.

KANE. Get what…?

MAYA (*offstage*). Felix is crying.

XANDER. Felix!

He goes to a door, there's nowhere to run to.

ENTERTAINER. Knock knock.

KANE. Get what?!

XANDER. I…

The ENTERTAINER *enters.*

ENTERTAINER. Sorry to bother you, Bea.

BEA. It's never a bother. Do you want a cup of tea?

ENTERTAINER. No, you're alright. It's just a quick one. I'll be quicker than a cat up a tree full of mice.

BEA. Is everything alright?

ENTERTAINER. I haven't heard from Alex.

BEA. Oh. Right.

ENTERTAINER. And, with you two being as entwined as you are, I was wondering what he's been up to? I just want to know that he's okay.

BEA.…

He's loving it, he's really enjoying his lectures, he says all his teachers are proper geniuses and he's learning so much.

ENTERTAINER. That is brilliant.

BEA. He's just been so busy studying for his exams.

ENTERTAINER. Time for fun too, I hope?

BEA. Oh yeah, he's been going to see loads of live music, and poetry nights.

ENTERTAINER. Poetry? Culture vulture now, eh?

BEA. He talks about you all the time when we speak.

ENTERTAINER. Yeah. Well. Thanks, love.

He leaves.

XANDER. I just didn't want to come home.

KANE. Why?

XANDER *shrugs*.

We were worried about you. It took up a lot of our energy.

XANDER. I'm sorry.

KANE. Okay.

XANDER. Bea, I am really sorry.

BEA. Yeah.

MAYA (*offstage*). Muuuuum!

BEA. Yes, love?

MAYA (*offstage*). Felix has stopped crying!

BEA. Great!

> *A beat.*

> Right. Are we good? Can we move on?

> *A fragile nod from* KANE.

XANDER. We were really close.

KANE. We were.

XANDER. I want to hear about you both, your life, your travels.

KANE. Yeah, let's make time for that.

> CELIA *enters.*

CELIA. You'll all be relieved to hear that Aonghy isn't concussed.

ALL. Great. / Phew. / Good news.

> DAVID *enters with drinks.*

DAVID. Time for a drink?

XANDER. Yes please!

DAVID. Clear Head for you?

XANDER. Absolutely not.

DAVID. Ciders for all, then!

> *They all grab a drink.*

BEA. I just want to say, it's been just as horrible as I thought it would be having all of you in my house!

> *Hahahaha.*

KANE. To old friends.

CELIA. And new!

BEA. Cheers.

ALL. Cheers!

SIMONE *appears. Everyone jumps. She pulls her hair back from her face.*

SIMONE. Why is it so quiet? Where are all the children?

BEA. They're watching *Encanto*.

SIMONE. I fell asleep in your garden. In a flower bed.

BEA. Oh. Are you okay?

SIMONE. No. It was nice. She was feeding the whole time. A caterpillar crawled on my arm. Can I –

She takes a bottle.

She passes KANE her baby.

She downs the cider.

She walks downstage.

Can I have a microphone, please?

The ENTERTAINER *brings her a microphone.*

Over the course of her speech, slowly slowly music starts; it builds stronger and stronger.

The ensemble become kids and adults simultaneously, and perform an abstracted ritual of transformation.

The mayfly spends most of its life beneath the surface of the water, waiting. Years. Then it hatches, lives for a day and dies.

A tadpole grows legs and lungs and becomes something that can leave the water. It loses its tail.

A snake sheds its skin. Leaves behind a perfect, translucent version of itself.

There's a fungus that infects ants. It takes over their bodies, makes them climb to the highest point they can find, clamp their jaws around a leaf, and wait. Then it grows out of their heads.

A starfish can lose a limb and grow it back. Sometimes the limb grows a whole new starfish.

Cells in the body are constantly dying. Replacing themselves. Your skin is not the same skin you had seven years ago. Your bones are not the same bones.

There is a moment where something ends. And you don't notice it at the time. There is a before, and then, later, you realise you are in an after.

Caterpillars dissolve inside the chrysalis. Completely. They don't just grow wings. They break themselves down until they form a kind of liquid. And then they rearrange themselves.

There are cells inside them already, that know what they are becoming. They survive the dissolution process. They turn the liquid into something with delicate, ornate wings, paper-thin and fluttering.

A body you have known your entire life, quietly and without asking permission, begins to change its shape. Soft tissue accumulates. Blood arrives. Hormones begin conducting experiments in mood, desire, anger.

Your skeleton stretches. Your skin breaks out.

Inside your abdomen, an entirely separate organism begins constructing itself out of your nutrients.

Your bones soften.

Your organs rearrange themselves.

Your blood volume increases by nearly fifty per cent.

There is another heartbeat inside you.

Two nervous systems.

Two circulatory systems.

Two skeletons.

At some point the body becomes a shared space.

An organism growing inside the host, feeding from its bloodstream, eventually tearing its way out.

And then something even stranger happens.

The body does not return to its previous state.

It becomes something else entirely.

Breasts become food. Sleep disappears.

Hormones reorganise themselves again.

The brain physically rewires around the presence of this other human being.

Which is perhaps why mothers can hear a child cough three rooms away through two closed doors while asleep.

The brain has literally changed its architecture.

Flesh mutates, swells, ruptures.

Skin splitting open.

Limbs bending the wrong way.

Orifices widening beyond recognition.

The body slips out from my control.

I think about that. Those caterpillars. The cells that know. I think about the version of me that existed before. Whether she's still in there. Somewhere.

Or whether she dissolved.

XANDER, *extremely drunk, stumbles through the streets. He gets out his phone.*

XANDER. Captain's log three a.m., twenty-eighth of June, Captain Xander is a drunkman.

'Twas but an accident. I had a shandy. But it's good, it's good, I feel really good.

I miss you. I'm so glad we're not like these people. How do you do this every weekend? It's suffocating!

Celia and David are such a bunch of posing poshos. Ooh, community! Ooh, my son is a model! Ooh, lah-di-dah. We're winners, you're a loser.

And Bea! She's just been in the same place all these years. Do you know that she lives just around the corner from her parents? All the stuff in her house is the same as when we were teenagers. She says 'I love my life' but I don't get it. I don't understand how she's okay with it. She just lives in this tiny world and she just doesn't fucking get it. She could have been somebody. She could have been so much more. But she's just turned out to be…

He makes a fart sound.

Anyway, it's weird being back. I feel like I'm a kid again, I keep seeing him everywhere.

Okayyyyy. I'm safe. I'm okay. I'm a balloon. I'm a bubble. I'm nobodyyyyy. G'bye. See you soon. All the best. Wish me luck. Byeeeee.

ENTERTAINER. Shhhhhhh.

XANDER *sleeps.*

PARTY THREE

The WhatsApp

XANDER*'s phone rings. He fumbles around and picks it up.*

XANDER. Mmm?

MARGOT. Xander?

XANDER. Mmm-hmm.

MARGOT. Are you asleep?

XANDER. Oh, no, no.

MARGOT. Big night or something?

XANDER. Hahahahahaha. Yep.

MARGOT. Listen, I don't want to alarm you, but we have a couple of problems.

XANDER. What?

MARGOT. My flight's delayed, I'll still make it but it'll be tight. I feel awful.

XANDER. It's okay, it's not your fault.

MARGOT. So it's all under control?

XANDER. Uh-huh.

MARGOT. So everything's ready?

XANDER. Um… Yes. I'm just finishing it all off.

MARGOT. Decorations?

XANDER. Yup.

MARGOT. Party bags?

XANDER. Oh yeah.

MARGOT. Cake?

XANDER. In the oven, as we speak.

MARGOT. Well, get you!

XANDER. Daddy's taking control!

MARGOT. That's great, Xand.

XANDER. Don't sound so surprised.

MARGOT. Quite sexy actually.

XANDER. We'll be fine.

MARGOT. Okay. Well. Well done. I'm proud of you.

XANDER. Thanks. I miss you.

MARGOT. Let me talk to him.

XANDER (*calling out*). Felix? Uh, Felix? (*To* MARGOT.) Ah. Yes. He's not here.

MARGOT. Where is he?

XANDER....He's... staying with David and Celia.

MARGOT. Is he?

XANDER. Yeah, no. That is definitely what is happening. Sleepover!

MARGOT. Really? I didn't think that Felix liked Aonghus that much.

XANDER. Yeah, they're best friends.

MARGOT. Okay, well. There's another thing.

XANDER. Mmm.

MARGOT. I saw you got added to the WhatsApp group.

XANDER. Oh god, I know.

MARGOT. You left a voicenote on there last night. At three forty-six a.m.

XANDER. What?

MARGOT. I haven't listened to it properly yet, but I'm guessing you didn't mean to do that. You might want to take a look.

XANDER. I'll call you back.

MARGOT. Yep.

He plays it back. Classical music plays. He starts hyperventilating. His phone buzzes.

XANDER. I feel like I'm gonna be sick.

MARGOT. What did you say?

XANDER. Nobody's said anything. It's nine-thirty and nobody's said anything. It's been on there for six hours, why isn't anybody saying anything?

MARGOT. Maybe they haven't seen it.

XANDER. Of course they've fucking seen it.

MARGOT. Don't swear at me.

XANDER. Fuck!

He hangs up. Then he throws up.

The phone beeps.

It's Bea. Oh shit shit shit.

A WhatsApp message from BEA.

BEA. We need to talk.

XANDER. What does that mean? What does that mean?!?!

The ensemble enter as part of 'The Elite Mummies (and Daddies) Club' WhatsApp group.

DAVID. Ooooh dear!

XANDER. Piss off, David!

CELIA. Xander, it's quite clear this message was sent in error.

DAVID. After a shandy or six!

CELIA. But this absolutely does not conform to our kindness policy, see description ☝. (*Index finger pointing up emoji.*)

XANDER. Look, I'm so sorry.

CELIA. As admin of this group I do feel like I have to say, publicly, that you have let down our community and upset many of our members with your careless words. However, given that our children will be in school together for many more years, and it's Felix's special day, I propose we agree to let sleeping dogs lie and try and enjoy the rest of this weekend.

DAVID. 👍 *(Thumbs-up emoji.)*

SIMONE. 👍 *(Thumbs-up emoji.)*

XANDER. 👍 *(Thumbs-up emoji.)*

CELIA. Bea?

Bea?

BEA. Do you need us to bring anything today?

XANDER. No – thank you.

BEA/CELIA/DAVID/SIMONE. 👍 *(Thumbs-up emoji.)*

They exit. DAVID *enters, privately messaging* XANDER.

DAVID. Heeeey, trooper.

XANDER. Hi, David.

DAVID. I told you not to join the WhatsApp group. Quite the bomb you dropped in there.

XANDER. Yeah.

DAVID. Absolute clanger.

XANDER. Uh-huh.

DAVID. What do they call that, again? Oh yeah that's it, social suicide.

XANDER. Ha.

DAVID. Ha ha. I wouldn't worry about it, we have a drama like that every week.

XANDER. Really?

DAVID. No, that is probably the worst one we've ever had.

XANDER. Haha.

DAVID. Haha.

XANDER. So is he doing alright?

DAVID.…Who?

XANDER. Uh, my son. Felix?

DAVID. Uh, I don't know, mate. That's a big question. You know him better than me, I suppose.

XANDER. He is at your house, right?

DAVID. Sorry?

XANDER. Sleepover?

DAVID. Oh, no. I don't think him and Aonghus are that close to be honest? I can check upstairs.

KANE *enters.*

KANE. Bro.

DAVID. One sec!

XANDER. Alright?

DAVID *exits.*

KANE. I'm not okay.

XANDER. What's going on?

KANE. What the hell happened last night?

XANDER. I'm not sure.

DAVID *re-enters.*

DAVID. Nope, he's not here.

XANDER. Really? He's not with Aonghus?

DAVID. Must be with someone else. Maybe ask on the group?

XANDER. Are you mental?

DAVID. I could ask for you?

XANDER. No, that's alright, David. I've found him. He's just here. No worries.

DAVID. Losing your own kid. You're hilarious, mate. Don't worry, your secret's safe with me.

XANDER. Haha thanks.

DAVID. Right, I'm off for a five K. See you later at your partay 🙏. (*Palms together emoji.*)

He exits.

KANE. I woke up with all my clothes on.

XANDER. Yeah, me too.

DAVID *reenters briefly.*

DAVID. Also accept me on Strava, you absolute nonce 🤡! (*Clown face emoji.*)

He exits.

KANE. Uuhh, the hangxiety is real.

XANDER. I hear you.

KANE. I had to escape. What am I doing with my life, man?

XANDER *frantically looks around his house.*

XANDER. Felix?

KANE. I'm thirty-three years old, I'm as old as Jesus was when he died.

XANDER. Feeelix?

KANE. Maybe I've got it wrong? Maybe there's an empty hole in the centre of my being. Maybe that's what the ayahuasca was trying to tell me?

XANDER. Listen, I know Bea probably doesn't want to speak to me right now but Felix isn't in my house and –

CELIA *enters.*

CELIA. Xander.

XANDER. Jesus! Celia.

KANE. You need help?

XANDER. What kind of help?

KANE. Psychiatric help.

CELIA. I just wanted to say…

XANDER. Probably haha. No, it's just that – you haven't seen Felix this morning, have you? At Bea's?

CELIA. What you said in the voicenote.

KANE. Why would he be at Bea's? He's your kid.

XANDER. Like a sleepover? Did you see him?

CELIA. It really upset me.

XANDER. Whoa fuck.

CELIA. I've tried really hard to make friends and put positive energy into our community and you mocked that.

XANDER. I'm so sorry, I was drunk. I really appreciate you ♥. (*Heart emoji.*)

KANE. No. I didn't see Felix. Not since last night.

XANDER. Fuck! So he's not at Bea's house?

KANE. Didn't look like it.

XANDER. Don't tell Bea. It'll just add insult to injury.

KANE. All good. Byeeeeeee.

KANE *exits.*

CELIA. And the term you used, to describe us, 'poshos'.

XANDER. HEEEEEELP!

CELIA. Needs some unpacking.

XANDER. Yeah.

CELIA. David's grandparents arrived from Hungary as refugees during the Second World War.

XANDER. I'm sorry to hear that.

CELIA. And though my mother's father was a rich man. (He invented the non-iron shirt.)

XANDER. Okay.

CELIA. He gambled it all away. And even before that, he was
very adamant she make her own way.

XANDER. Okay.

CELIA. She was on benefits for a period when we were
growing up. Had to grow her own potatoes in the garden.

XANDER. Okay.

CELIA. Just thought it was best you were informed.

XANDER. Sorry for the confusion.

CELIA. I'm sorry too. Here's an article if you want to educate
yourself further.

She chucks a massive book at him.

Still ten o'clock at yours?

XANDER. Yeah.

CELIA. 👍 *(Thumbs-up emoji.)*

CELIA *exits.* XANDER *opens the book.*

BOOK. '*Why 'Posh' is Problematic: The Microaggression
Nobody's Talking About.*'

He closes it and chucks it away.

XANDER. Ahhhhh!

BEA *enters.*

Listen, Bea. I hope you're doing okay.

BEA. Morning! You've given me a lot to reflect on, Xander.

XANDER. Oh. Oh.

BEA. But here's something I thought you might find interesting.

She chucks a book at his head.

XANDER. Ow!

He opens it.

BOOK. '*How To Stop Being a Narcissist: An Idiot's Guide to Taking Control of Your Own Toxic Traits.*'

BEA *leaves.*

XANDER (*he drafts and redrafts his message*). Bea, Celia, David, everyone, look, I just wanted to say, about the voicenote…

That was insane, you know I obviously don't think that…

I should explain…

Have you seen Felix, I've lost him. I'm terrified…

Oh, whoops!…

Ahh!… Never mind.

Everyone enters.

CELIA. Hi, everyone, it's me, the posing posho! Haha kidding, just kidding. A friendly reminder about next Saturday's Wellness Fair for Sprogs! This is an opportunity…

XANDER *skips to the end of message.*

…meditation for tots! We are still in need of volunteers for the day and additional funds, so I've just popped the donation link below 👇 . (*Index finger pointing down emoji.*)

XANDER*'s phone rings.*

XANDER. Hello.

MARGOT. You hung up on me.

XANDER. Margot.

MARGOT. You swore at me and then you hung up the phone.

XANDER. Margot –

MARGOT. You do not swear at me, okay?

XANDER. Look, I'm just a bit stressed right now, okay?

MARGOT. And why the hell did you say that? ON THE GROUP. What you do impacts my life. What you do impacts our son's life! I hold a lot of this together, Xander. I can't also be the person you kick when it starts slipping. When you talk to me like that you sound so common.

XANDER. Margot, I'm sorry but… Hang on, what did you just say?

MARGOT. I'm boarding the plane now – we'll continue this conversation later.

XANDER. I think I'm going to be sick again.

He runs to the bathroom. Everyone enters. CELIA *is typing on* DAVID*'s phone.*

DAVID. Hi Celia, Thanks for the details about the wellness fair. I shall certainly be attending! With bells on! 🔔 (*Bells emoji.*) (Even if I didn't happen to be married to the fabulous woman organising it!)

Also, I'm so sorry that our son is so beautiful and charismatic that he was headhunted by a modelling agency, and I really do regret any unpleasant feelings that that might be bringing up for members of this group.

KANE. No need to apologise about your son's natural talents, Dave. I sense the universe has plans for him.

CELIA. Kane, what are you doing here?

KANE. David added me. I like to stay informed.

All exit.

XANDER. Hi Simone.

SIMONE *re-enters. She doesn't respond. Wind sound plays.*

I think we met yesterday. Our kids are friends. I was the guy with the beanie?

Just a quick one from me.

Just checking in. My Felix is at your place, right? Sleepover?

Fun sleepover with Dante?

Simone?

The doorbell rings. KANE *arrives.*

KANE. I think I've realised – I need to have a child. It is the only thing that will give my life meaning.

XANDER. Right. Maybe now isn't a good time.

KANE. Where's your son?

XANDER. Felix?

KANE. Yeah. 'Felix.'

XANDER. Uh… Uh…

KANE. Have you lost him? Have you lost your son?! Fucking hell. The most precious thing! You idiot! You fucking idiot!

XANDER. This is all your fault! We got too drunk.

KANE. I'm not a father, Alex. This is on you. I'm going to search the perimeter.

Felix!!!

He dives out the window.

XANDER. Kane?

BEA *enters.*

BEA. Me again.

XANDER. Bea.

BEA. Can I just say, you should probably reflect on your life choices and, I don't know, grow up. It's kind of a dick move slagging me off.

XANDER. Bea –

BEA. You can't look down on me from your high horse when you literally live round the corner, you walking talking definition of gentrification, you matcha-slurping, micro-beanie-wearing twat.

Everyone enters.

DAVID. Hi all, Celia and I are looking to sell some of our art. Let us know if interested.

Scrolls.

CELIA. Together with some other loony parents I'm walking the entire coast of Dorset (over ninety miles) in three-point-five days in September.

Scrolls.

BEA. Anyone have a boy's jacket Maya could borrow for John Darling in *Peter Pan*?

Scrolls.

CELIA. PS so far only managed ten K before my feet started hurting and knee swelled up… *(Flushed face emoji. Grimacing face emoji.)*

Scrolls.

DAVID. Hi all, FYI we have some good availability for our chalet in Bude over August, do let us know if interested. *(Smiling face emoji.)*

Scrolls.

SIMONE. My nipples are very raw – any tips?

Scrolls.

KANE. Any homeopathic remedies for prolonging my fertility? *(Aubergine emoji.)*

CELIA. Hi. If anyone is looking for a cleaner my 'ray of sunshine' is looking for more work. *(Broom emoji.)*

The ENSEMBLE *begin overlapping their text, in a rising, increasingly intense deluge of banal messages, until they are cut off by* XANDER.

XANDER. Oh who cares!!

DAVID.…Xander?

XANDER. I need your help. Someone? Please help me! I've lost my son! I got drunk and I lost him. I haven't seen him since last night and I don't know where he is. I'm a terrible person. I'm a terrible father.

CELIA. Oh my god.

DAVID. Jesus. You said –

XANDER. I lied. He's gone!

CELIA. Oh my god!

DAVID. How could you do that?

What's wrong with you?

KANE. He's not anywhere on the perimeter!

DAVID. The perimeter of what?

CELIA. Wow. Bad father alert!

DAVID. Celia. Don't shame him.

CELIA. Sorry, wrong chat.

KANE. That is pretty fucked up to be honest.

XANDER. Please help me! Please!

BEA. Everyone stop!

Hands on your heads. Hands on your shoulders.

Hands on your knees. Shoulders, heads and sssshhhh.

Now, I've just called the police.

David, Celia, we were all pissed last night, so talk to Aonghus and see if he knows what happened.

CELIA/DAVID. 👍 (*Thumbs-up emoji.*)

DAVID *and* CELIA *leave.*

BEA. Simone, contact the wider PTA network, we'll set up a search party.

SIMONE. 👍 (*Thumbs-up emoji.*)

SIMONE *leaves.*

BEA. KANE! COME HOME NOW. If you're going to stay in my house you need to help with childcare.

KANE. Fair enough 👍😎. (*Thumbs-up emoji. Sunglasses emoji.*)

KANE *leaves.*

BEA. Xander, stay calm, sit tight, and don't do anything stupid. He's a clever boy. He knows your name, your phone number and his address. It's going to be okay.

XANDER. I don't think it is, Bea, I've got a bad feeling about this.

BEA *leaves.*

Someone? Anyone? Dad?

The ENTERTAINER *enters. He conjures a table, chairs, two cups of tea and a box of biscuits. They sit.*

ENTERTAINER. So what seems to be the problem?

XANDER. I've lost my son.

ENTERTAINER. And I've lost my keys. So that makes us both a couple of scatterbrains!

XANDER. You're not listening, I've lost Felix.

ENTERTAINER. And find him you shall. But let's deal with you first.

XANDER. What about me?

ENTERTAINER. Why don't you try to tell me what's wrong?

XANDER. I don't know.

ENTERTAINER. Name the problem, and then maybe I can help you fix it.

XANDER. I feel…

ENTERTAINER. Good start. You feel…

XANDER. A bit…

ENTERTAINER. A bit…

XANDER. Shaky.

ENTERTAINER. Shaky.

XANDER. Angry.

ENTERTAINER. Angry.

XANDER. Scared.

ENTERTAINER. Scared.

XANDER. Unanchored.

ENTERTAINER. Unanchored.

XANDER. At sea.

ENTERTAINER. At sea.

XANDER. Untethered.

ENTERTAINER. Untethered.

XANDER. Ashamed.

ENTERTAINER. Ashamed?

XANDER. Ashamed.

ENTERTAINER. Ashamed.

XANDER. Yes.

ENTERTAINER. Ashamed of what?

XANDER. My life. Who I was. You. You mainly.

    You living this shit life.

    There's this whole world out there that you didn't know about and that you didn't get. You didn't understand. And you were okay with that.

    You were so happy with just being you.

    But you were a nothing person, trying to be a something person. And that was painful to watch. To see you make an idiot of yourself, whilst the other kids mocked you – you know they mocked you? They used to call you the Magic Plasterer.

    That was so –

    And then Felix was born and all of this stuff grew and mutated and I didn't know what to do with it. And then you died before I could talk to you about any of it. So now it's just this huge disgusting thing that I can't make right with you because you're gone now.

    Think that's it.

ENTERTAINER. What a lot of feelings for one little chap.

XANDER. I'm so sorry. I'm sorry, Dad.

ENTERTAINER. You're my boy. You're my boy and you always will be.

The Magnificent Alexander Tertainer!

XANDER. How are you not angry at me?

ENTERTAINER. I remember when you got your letter from the university. I remember the expression on your face. There must have been lightbulbs in that envelope because you were just… illuminated. I watched as your world expanded before my very eyes. It was mesmerising.

I never got a magic envelope, mate. I had to work out how to expand my own world.

Do you know how I feel? When I put on this costume?

XANDER. No.

ENTERTAINER. Invincible.

When I step out on that stage, and those kids clap and cheer, and I know the memory I've just helped them make will last a lifetime, that is what the hokey cokey's all about. And if I raise some eyebrows along the way, well…

He shrugs.

I'm light as a feather, kid. You're stiff as a board. You're an overinflated balloon. Pardon my French, but it seems to me you are filled to the brim with guff. It's taking you away from what's important.

Pull my finger.

XANDER *pulls the* ENTERTAINER*'s finger. An old bell chimes.*

Time to go, I reckon. Don't you?

XANDER. Yeah.

ENTERTAINER. One last magic trick?

Folks, this one's an ancient spell, as old as time itself. This one is magic. Pure magic.

It's called 'The Final Act of Vanishing'. It's a hell of a finisher, in which the magician vanishes into thin air, once and for all, everything that has been weighing him down. And it's permanent, and it's irreversible and it can be painful. And it can only be performed by…

XANDER *raises his hand.*

What's your name?

XANDER. Alexander Tertainer.

ENTERTAINER. What's your name?

XANDER. Alexander Tertainer. And I'm thirty-four-and-a-half years old.

ENTERTAINER. Thirty-four-and-a-half years old! Big round of applause for Alex Tertainer. Yeah, crowd goes wild!

ENTERTAINER *hands* XANDER *his magic wand.*

You ready, mate?

XANDER. Yeah, I think so.

The ENTERTAINER *holds* XANDER.

ENTERTAINER. Break a leg.

The ENTERTAINER *gets out a 'magic sheet' made out of the same material as Binky.*

He stands in the door.

The ENTERTAINER *covers the doorway with the sheet.*

XANDER *raises the wand and the sheet rises.*

Knock knock.

XANDER. Who's there?

No response.

The sheet drops. The ENTERTAINER *is gone, only his hat remains.* XANDER *picks up the hat.*

Felix?

FELIX (*offstage crying*). Daddy?

XANDER. Felix?

FELIX (*offstage crying*). Daddy!

XANDER. Felix, where are you?

FELIX (*offstage crying*). I'm in the airing cupboard.

XANDER *gets him and carries him onstage.*

XANDER. It's okay, mate, shhh it's okay. What were you doing in the airing cupboard?

FELIX. I was doing my magic trick and I couldn't get out and then I fell asleep and then I didn't know where I was.

XANDER. You told me you could disappear, didn't you?

FELIX. Yeah.

XANDER. And you did! You did so well. Maybe don't do it for quite so long next time, okay?

FELIX. Okay.

XANDER. I missed you.

XANDER *hugs him.*

Do you want Binky?

FELIX. Yeah.

He gives him Binky.

XANDER. Knock knock.

FELIX. Who's there?

XANDER. Who.

FELIX. Who who?

XANDER. What's it like to be an owl?

They laugh.

Okay, monster, do you want to go and get ready for your party?

FELIX. Yeah.

XANDER. Go and get your costume on.

>XANDER *gives* FELIX *the wand.* FELIX *exits.*

Hey, everyone.

The ensemble return.

Me again.

I've found him.

He's here.

He was just doing a magic trick.

He's safe.

He's with me.

Look, I'm aware I've made a really bad impression this weekend. Historically bad. I said some really shitty things on here and I need to apologise to some of you. Most of you. All of you.

Felix's birthday party is still on and I need your help. I thought I could just blag it but, surprise surprise, I can't. I need you. All of you. Doing this without support doesn't really work, does it?

I can see there's a number of you lurking in this WhatsApp group who I haven't met. It would be good to chat, get to know you better.

So you're all invited to my house. My door is open. I really hope you can make it.

The focus changes from XANDER *to his fellow parents.*

A message dings.

Fin.

www.nickhernbooks.co.uk

@nickhernbooks